3-9-76

MANUAL FOR LECTORS

Judith Tate

Pflaum Publishing
Dayton, Ohio

Library of Congress Catalog
Card Number: 75-23848
ISBN: 0-8278-0030-4

Printed in the United States of America.

CONTENT

The Role of the Lector

Understanding Scripture

Work Sheets for Lectors

Commissioning Lectors

THE ROLE OF THE LECTOR

LECTOR AS MINISTER

One of Red Skelton's skits has him delivering a powerful speech using only the ABCs as text. En route to a meeting, he mistakenly picks up his small son's penmanship paper. When he is called upon to deliver his talk, he strides to the speaker's platform, unfolds his paper, is momentarily horrified, and then rallies.

"A, B," he begins. He picks up power: "C, D, E, F." He shakes a finger and proclaims: "G, H, and J, K, L!" He pleads, thunders, chides, questions, and laments several times through the alphabet. His finish is triumphant.

We recognize in the Skelton skit the common experience of being moved more by the sound of words than by their sense. Empty rhetoric, of course, has no staying power. It does not clarify a person's values or sustain a person in any conversion of heart. That is why, even in the purely secular realm, really good speech requires sense as well as sound, conviction as well as skill.

The lector is required to combine faith and skill when he reads the Scriptures. Together with his brother, the priest, the lector is a minister. Both ministries are responsible for effecting the presence of God among Christians gathered in worship. Just as the priest effects the special presence of God in the Eucharist, the lector effects God's special presence in his scriptural word. So both priest and lector are ministers to the Christian community.

This concept of ministry is extremely important for lectors. Without it, they may see themselves simply as performers before a captive audience. In a way, of course, they do have a special role in the religious drama called Eucharist. They even have "scripts" and movement "cues," and they are called on to employ public speaking skills. But they are not performers. They are servants.

To be a minister means to be a servant, to serve the people.

Too often the meaning of God's scriptural word remains locked in expressionless, monotonous reading. When that happens, the people not only are subjected to dullness of style but are cheated of God's full message to them. But when a lector opens the Scriptures and sounds God's word with faith and feeling and sensitive skill, he heightens its meaning. That kind of reading is truly a service to the people. God, of course, is present regardless of the personal style of a minister. But the reality of God's presence can be made plainer and stronger when the style of the ministry is fine and full of faith.

The Scriptural Word makes the Lord present in a way analogous to the way his historical Body is made present in the Eucharist.

Hans Urs von Balthasar

LECTOR IN HISTORY

From the very beginning of the church, the ministry of lectors was distinct from that of celebrants. One reason for this separation of ministries was that most early Christians were Jews who were used to the separate customs of Temple and Synagogue. Priests offered sacrifice; lectors read the Scriptures. Those Jewish Christians simply carried these two separate ministries over into their Christian worship.

Another reason for the special office of lector was that, in the early church, the people chose their ministers according to their special talents. Those with a talent for reading God's word with special grace were elected to do just that.

Since people always have had an inclination to ritualize important events, the early Christians very quickly created special rituals of ordination for their ministers. In the ritual for ordaining priests, the bishop laid hands on the ordinands. In the ritual for ordaining lectors, the bishop handed over a book of the Scriptures. By the time Hippolytus wrote *The Apostolic Tradition* in the third century, these ordination rites already were customary. Hippolytus wrote: "The reader is appointed by the bishop's handing to him the Book. For he does not have hands laid upon him."

Like priests and deacons, lectors were bound by their appointment to a particular local church to serve the people who had chosen them. Lectors, along with deacons and acolytes, were said to have "minor orders" — not because their services were unimportant but because they differed from what always has been the major service of the church: presiding over the Eucharistic table.

In some places, there were as many as eight minor orders. These orders in the very early church were open to women as well as to men. Election was based on the person's talent for service, not on his rank or sex. In time, attitude and custom changed. Women gradually were banned from liturgical service. And lectors gave up their ministry to higher-ranking priests or deacons. The office of lector as special minister virtually came to be nonexistent. The general custom in the West came to be that the priest-celebrant stood at the altar with his back toward the people, and he read God's word only in Latin. This custom lasted for centuries.

Then, in 1958, Pius XII encouraged lay persons again to take part in the liturgy, primarily as commentators. This restoration caused a stir. Even in more progressive parishes, lay commentators at first were asked to remain outside the sanctuary. But at least this was a step toward restoration of the lay persons' rightful role in ministry to the people and in the public worship of God.

Following Pius XII's lead, church leaders at Vatican Council II fully restored the function not only of commentator but also of lector as genuine ministries. Now lay persons — women and men — not only come into the sanctuary to read, but they proclaim the word from the same pulpit that the priest uses. This practice demonstrates the unity of the word proclaimed by priest and by lay person in complementary roles.

Lectors and commentators ... also exercise a genuine liturgical ministry. They ought, therefore, to discharge their office with the sincere piety and decorum demanded by so exalted a ministry.

Liturgy, *Vatican II*

LECTOR IN MEDITATION

The first principle of good speech communication is this: *Know what you are talking about.* And the second is like it: *Believe in what you are saying.*

If a lector is a person called to make God present in a special way among his people, then it is important not only for the lector but also for the people that he or she both *know* and *believe* God's word. That takes more than a five-minutes-before-Mass reading. In fact, it takes more than reading; it takes meditating. This meditating needs to be *in*-formed — that is, formed from within. That requires knowledge and study.

Meditative study helps one discover the interior meaning of the word. The meaning includes not only the literal sense of a passage but also its form and mood and context; all of this combined completes the meaning. Getting to the heart of a reading in this way is a form of meditation, or meditative study.

We depend a great deal these days on "process." So it might be helpful here to describe a simple, four-step process for meditative study. We will use a passage from Jeremiah 10:1-7 as an example.

First step. Pray. A simple prayer serves to remind the lector that he or she is a religious minister and that the Book is God's word. Here might be an example of good preparatory prayer: "God, my Father, I do believe that you are present in this Book that I hold here in my hands. Help me to read your word with faith. Help me to understand it and to communicate it to your people."

Second step. Find out the context and the literary form of the reading (see page 14ff). One good way to discover the context is to read the entire chapter from which the passage comes. Many Bibles also have an introduction at the beginning of each book.

Preparing to read the Jeremiah passage, for instance, one would find that this youthful prophet lived at a time when the Hebrews had lapsed into a shallow, hypocritical, and even idolatrous religious life. Many Hebrews even sacrificed children to the pagan god Moloch and took part in the fertility cults of Baal. Jeremiah called for a purified religion and for social justice. He was, of course, unpopular. He was threatened, mocked, imprisoned in a muddy cistern, exiled, and probably murdered in exile. His life in many ways foreshadowed Jesus' life. Knowing these details about Jeremiah should help a lector to read his prophecies with greater sensitivity.

Third step. Read the passage slowly, thoughtfully. Determine the mood or tone. This particular passage from Jeremiah, for instance, is a poem. It is written in a tone of warning but also of praise.

Fourth step. Break the passage into thought units, then write your thoughts on each unit. For example:

Hear the word which the Lord speaks to you, O house of Israel. Thus says the Lord:

A good reminder that this is the word from the Lord. Boggles my imagination. I must read this with power. Thunder.

Learn not the customs of the nations, and have no fear of the signs of the heavens, though the nations fear them.

Nations = pagan nations. Signs of heavens = superstitions. If we really believe in God, we won't be afraid of our "stars". Astrology, etc. Funny how appropriate it is today - 2500 years later!

For the cult idols of the nations are nothing, wood cut from the forest, wrought by craftsmen with tools, adorned with silver and gold.

False gods have no power at all. They don't even have existence till men give it to them. I wonder how many times I've given existence to a false god.

7

With nails and hammers they are
fastened, that they may not totter.
Like a scarecrow in a cucumber field
are they, they cannot speak;

They must be carried about, for
they cannot walk.

Fear them not, they can do no
harm, neither is it in their power
to do good.

No one is like you, O Lord,
great are you, great and mighty
is your name.

Who would not fear you,
king of the nations, for it is
your due!

Jeremiah makes the false gods seem ludicrous. I guess those who believe in them are also ludicrous — if they've once known you, God.

They can't harm us. But we can harm ourselves by believing in them.

Mood changes. Must change my voice. This is praise. And awe.

You are King — even of "pagan" nations. And King of this parish — and of me. Fear? = Awe, respect, love, awareness of your power and your goodness.

Think of the faith that could be enlivened in your parish if your priest-minister and all your lector-ministers
were filled each Sunday with such understanding, with
vigorous faith, with a deeply personal response to the
presence of God *in* him and *through* him! *In* the assem-
bly of believers.

**What I tell you in
darkness, speak in
the light. What you
hear in private, pro-
claim from the
housetops.**

Matthew 10:27

LECTOR BEFORE THE PEOPLE

Even a strong man's knees can become watery at the
thought that there he stands . . . before all those people!
And yet, standing there is part of being a lector. Lectors
are seen before they are heard. So it might be wise here
to discuss the appearance of lectors.

Consideration of appearance brings up a question of
style: What does the modern lector wear? In some parishes, it is customary to wear some kind of robe or stole.
In others, regular lay clothing is preferred. Those who
prefer a distinctive garb maintain that, since others in
the sanctuary wear vestments, it makes for an orderliness
or congruity when lectors also wear some special vest-
ment-like clothing. Furthermore, they contend that,
since lectors are real ministers called from the congregation for a distinct liturgical function, a stole or robe is a
fitting way to show this special role.

Some people maintain, on the other hand, that wearing lay clothing is a good way to indicate that the lector
is a lay minister. It also is pointed out that currently the
church is trying to simplify many vestments and rituals,
so a new addition might be inappropriate.

Lectors, ideally, should come from among those par-
ishioners who would find neither custom upsetting.
They simply should know the custom of their parish,
understand the reasons for that custom, and be com-
fortable in whatever they are wearing.

Dress is not as essential to a lector's appearance as are
posture and movement. According to experts on body
language, we communicate disdain, friendliness, insecuri-
ty, suppressed anger, welcome, and many other positive
and negative feelings by the way we hold our heads or by
what we do with our hands or by our manner of sitting,
standing, or walking. Lectors who are overly preoccupied
with their position "up there before all those people"
will likely communicate nervousness. They may walk
stiffly or stand with ducked head or choke the microphone.

The simplest — although not the easiest — rule governing posture is this: *Concentrate on the people and God's word to them instead of on yourself.* When God's message is really uppermost in a lector's mind, his or her body language will be natural and dignified. Some practical pointers may help maintain this natural dignity.

First, the microphone. Lectors should adjust the microphone to their own height *before* Mass so that the message does not begin during a testing period. Once it is adjusted, lectors should ignore the microphone. They are speaking to people, not to a microphone.

Second, the book. When reading, it is appropriate to hold the book on one palm with the other palm resting on top to keep the place and to help balance the book. This position enables the lector to see the book and also the people simply by shifting his gaze; there should be no need to duck the head. Too much head-ducking makes it seem that the lector is addressing the book rather than the people. It also causes the voice to be muffled. If a lectern or stand is used, simply rest the hands comfortably on the stand or on the open book.

Third, the people. Lectors should look at the people. If "knowing and believing what you say" is the first principle of communication, eye contact is the first practical skill. Lectors should try to look at the entire congregation — now here, now there, very smoothly. When a speaker is good at this practice, people feel he or she is talking right to them. That precisely is the point: God *is* speaking right to the people.

LECTOR SPEAKING

Lectors who study and meditate on the reading before-hand will find it easier to give good voice to God's word. Nervousness ordinarily will not be a problem. If ever it is, a few simple practices will help reduce or eliminate tension.

1. Inhale very slowly and very deeply. Pause between each breath.

2. Inhale, then direct your breath-energy into voice power. This will make the voice clear and strong. Once you hear your own strong voice, you will become more confident.

3. Take your time. Don't begin speaking until you have "breathed" yourself into a state of calm.

4. Speak slowly and deliberately; then you will *sound* confident — and that will help make you *feel* confident.

During the reading itself:

1. Wait for the people to be seated. Be still until they are looking at you.

2. Announce clearly the reading. If you want to make a comment to help people understand the reading, do it with assurance. Then pause again before the actual reading. The homily, of course, is the ideal place to develop the themes of the reading; but the lector can help by giving a brief preface to the reading.

3. Read slowly. Make each word distinct. Some speech coaches suggest "spitting" the final consonants because they are so often lost.

4. Make eye contact. This practice invites the attention of listeners, helps keep them alert.

5. For God's sake — or for the sake of his message — read with expression. If you are reading a story passage from Genesis, tell a good story. If you are reading a warning from a prophet, make it thunder. (The second portion of this manual will be helpful to you in this regard.)

Do people still complain of not being made to hear God's truth? If they do it is probably not because it has never been proposed to them, but rather because it has been spoken to them woodenly, perfunctorily, perhaps, and not with the vigor, care, and passion that His Truth demands.

James Turro

UNDERSTANDING SCRIPTURE

FIRST READINGS

Even with reflection and some speaking skill, a lector is
likely to find reading Scripture aloud difficult. One major reason for this difficulty is a failure to perceive the
literary form of a given Scriptural passage. If a lector,
for example, tries to read poetry as if it were law or history, no amount of good will, resonance, or diction will
salvage the message fully. Knowledge of the literary
form of a passage is a prerequisite for good reading. And
hints for reading the various forms is helpful if not essential. For these two reasons, we offer this simplified refer-
ence section.

First readings usually come from the Old Testament, and
they nearly always relate to a theme in the day's gospel.
Since the Old Testament books vary in form, they de-
mand a corresponding variation of expression.

It is important to note that the indicator list below is
greatly simplified. A book labeled *prophecy,* for example, may include fiction, sermon, vision, or biography.
So it will be necessary to check out the specific passage
to be read.

To use this aid, find the literary form of the day's
reading by referring to the alphabetized list below. Then
look under the appropriate literary-form section for suggestions about reading.

Book	Literary Form
Amos	prophecy
Baruch	prophecy
1 & 2 Chronicles	history
Daniel	apocalypse; biography
Deuteronomy	history; sermon; law
Ecclesiastes	wisdom sayings
Ecclesiasticus Also called *Sirach*	poetry (didactic)
Esther	fiction
Exodus	history; biography; laws
Ezekiel	prophecy
Ezra	history; memoirs
Genesis	myth; biography; history

Habakkuk	prophecy; poetry
Haggai	prophecy
Hosea	prophecy; biography; poetry
Isaiah	prophecy; poetry
Jeremiah	prophecy; history; biography
Job	poetry (dramatic)
Joel	prophecy
Jonah	fiction (didactic)
Joshua	history
Judges	biography; history
Judith	fiction
1& 2 Kings	history; biography
Lamentations	poetry (elegy)
Leviticus	law
1 & 2 Maccabees	history; biography
Malachi	prophecy
Micah	prophecy
Nahum	prophecy
Nehemiah	biography; sermon
Numbers	law; history
Obadiah	prophecy
Proverbs	poetry (didactic); sayings
Psalms	poetry (lyric); prayer
Ruth	biography (fictional)
1 & 2 Samuel	history; biography
Song of Songs	poetry (lyric)
Tobit	fiction
Wisdom	poetry (didactic); sayings
Zechariah	prophecy
Zephaniah	prophecy

LITERARY FORMS

Apocalyptic. Apocalyptic literature is highly symbolic. It usually speaks of past events as if they were future events. This is a unique way of showing how God's plan unfolds. It is as if, standing in the present time, someone writes as if he were in the 1950s. Such a writer might "predict" a past event in symbolic terms, something like this: Hundreds of red-robed horsemen (bishops) will call up gentle winds from the four corners of the earth (gathering of Vatican II Council), and the wind will become a storm (confusion resulting from the fast changes); but it will pass, leaving in its wake a delicately blooming bush (new life in the church).

Since most apocalyptic writing refers to specific historic events and is written in complex symbols, it is very difficult to understand. Thus, it is difficult to read aloud. Fortunately, not many readings are from apocalypses.

Suggestion: Try to capture in your voice the mood of the symbols. If the symbols indicate power and threat, read with power and threat in your voice. If they indicate awe, mystery, hope, try to put that into your voice. You can be dramatic in your expression, since this form of literature is so highly colored.

Biography. This form includes autobiography and fictionalized biography. Biography is a story of a real person. Scripture is peopled with all kinds of real historical persons — our spiritual ancestors. Like modern biography, these passages often are stranger than fiction, and they read like a good story.

Suggestion: Get acquainted with the subject of the reading. Was he or she a weak person or a strong one? Intelligent or slow-witted? Scalawag or a person of high integrity? When you read biographical passages aloud, stress phrases that point up the personality of the subject. Since these passages are about real persons, try to make them come alive right there in the gathering of the Christians who are listening to you.

Fiction. Scriptural fiction is among the most charming fiction in the world. It is often full of humor, irony, poetic justice. Sometimes it is full of pathos. Scriptural fiction always has a point. It may depict the ideal man or woman; it may show that good wins over evil; it may demonstrate that God will effect his plan despite the bungling interference of some people. Scripture makes these points in sermons, history, and other forms as well as in fiction. But when the point is made in story form, it should be read like a story, not like a sermon.

Suggestion: Put the mood of the story in your voice — gusto, pity, tenderness. Make the details clear. Change your voice for different characters in the story. Tobit, for example, does not sound like his wife, Anna. Make the personalities come alive. Charm your listeners.

History. Some historical accounts in Scripture are dry and factual. Others are full of color, movement, and larger-than-life characters. Most are "interpretive" — that is, the historian is not so much interested in the accuracy of dates or of other facts as he is in the *meaning* of the history. All Scripture is theology. The most constant meaning, or interpretation, was that God is the Lord of history: He has a plan, and that plan takes place in history in the lives of men.

Suggestion: Find out what kind of history best describes the passage you are reading. If it is factual, you may have to read it like a newscast. If it is more colorful, pick up and stress the phrases that give the passage life. Emphasize the *meaning,* when possible, by pausing and by changing your voice.

Law. Even the books dealing specifically with law and ritual are sometimes spiced with stories and anecdotes. In the passages that are strictly statements of law, try to see the calibre of the moral life of our Hebrew ancestors. In the ritual laws, try to note their concern for the proper worship of God and their sensitivity to symbol.

Suggestion: Proclaim the law passages with a clear, strong, no-nonsense voice. Be a lawgiver.

Memoirs. See *Biography* above.

Poetry.   Scriptural poetry ranges from aphorisms
to fine lyricism. One thing lectors should note about
Hebrew poetry is that it often says the same thing twice.
The effect of oral reading is better if the second statement is more like an emphasis echo than like a brand-
new thought. For instance, notice how the second lines
repeat the thought of the first lines in these verses:

    1   O God, hear my prayer;
    2   hearken to the words of my mouth.

    1   Behold: God is my helper;
    2   The Lord sustains my life.

The psalms used as responses to the first reading often
are read poorly because readers are not aware of this kind
of poetic parallelism.
   Suggestion: Since poetry is the most expressive literary form of all, put great expression into it, being alert
to parallelisms. *Dramatic* poetry has several speakers, as
in the book of Job. It is like a play. Change your voice
for the various characters. If the poetry is an *elegy,* capture the sadness in your voice. Read the poetry in a
slightly modulated tone, and make good use of pauses
for emphasis. If the poetry is *lyric,* let the mood of
praise or joy be caught in an excited voice as well as in
the words. Mood changes are swift in Hebrew poetry,
particularly in some psalms. Be sure to allow a pause between moods.

Prophecy.   Most prophets spoke when the Hebrews
were living in critical and confusing situations. Many
people mistakenly think the prophets' main task was to
predict the future in a fortune-telling sense. But, actually, their main task was to interpret the current situation.
Their predictions were more in the line of a call to re-
form: "If you do not repent and change, then this or
that evil will fall on you." The prophets tried to persuade the people to be loyal to God. That meant, among
other things, being just to fellowmen, being generous to

the poor, and being faithful in worship. Although the specific historical events do not apply to us, that prophetic call to loyalty to God applies today as much as it did in centuries past.

Suggestion: Get acquainted with the prophet you are reading; the prophets were unique, strong, and often strange individuals. Hosea, for instance, usually is gentle; Malachi usually is sarcastic; Amos is blunt, even crude. Nearly all of them spoke with thundering power. Make your words resound with vigor. Make the people feel as if the prophet were speaking right to them. In a way, he is.

Sermon. Many people consider sermons the dullest of all speech forms. (St. Teresa of Avila claims she never tired of sermons — "however bad they were"!) But a sermon truly can be rousing. Scriptural sermons often have the distinct flavor of the preacher.

Suggestion: Find out who the preacher of the sermon is and what the occasion is. Try to be there. Give a good sermon. Don't read the passage; preach it.

SECOND READINGS

Since the Holy Spirit speaks differently through different men — or through men at different times and in different situations — it is important for readers of Scripture to understand the style, mood, and thinking of the various writers. The following notes on New Testament books are extremely oversimplified. But they should be helpful in providing clues about the general spirit and hints for oral reading.

Acts of the Apostles. Acts is the only early account we have of the first years of the church. It was written about the year 75 by the same person who wrote the Gospel of Luke. It covers the first 30 years of the church after Jesus' death and resurrection. In literary form, Acts is a kind of transparent history with the action of God showing through. Luke is not just telling a chronological story of the church; he is showing how the church is the mystery of God, how the church was moved by the Spirit to open itself to the Gentiles and to the entire world.

The tone of reading should not be matter-of-fact; it should have a certain excitement or awe. It might be analogous to the way someone would tell an event in his life that contained a sense of miracle.

Colossians. Paul wrote this letter while in prison. It was probably an answer to a letter from Epaphras who had founded the church at Colossae. Evidently there were certain problems regarding angels, ascetical practices, and false teachers. Paul answers these questions. In general, however, the Christians at Colossae must have been strong and loyal, and the tone of the letter is complimentary and encouraging. This was one of Paul's last letters, written after he had spent years of hard work, suffering, and imprisonment. A gentler, mellowed Paul wrote this letter. He wrote in a tone of calm pride. It should be read in that tone.

I Corinthians. Paul himself says that he began his missionary work in Corinth "in weakness and fear, and with much trepidation." No wonder. Corinth had a reputation for being depraved and pagan. Sure enough, many problems arose in the church after he left there: a minority group split into cliques, some Christians took up religious prostitution and other pagan customs, some preached heretical doctrines, many quarreled even at the Eucharist. Even the more faithful majority had problems of conscience and of doctrine.

Paul addressed these struggling Christians in a voice of authority. He often made use of rhetorical questions and often answered himself. The letter contains a certain urgency, sometimes a frustration amounting to anger, and frequently a now-listen-to-me ring. It should be read in that same no-nonsense spirit, in a voice full of authority and yet full of pleading.

II Corinthians. One thing that makes this letter difficult to read — particularly to read aloud — is its choppiness or discontinuity. Some scholars believe that discontinuity results from the letter, as we have it, actually being a patch-work of several letters. Others think it results from Paul's fatigue and his worry about the community at Corinth. It certainly is Paul's most personal letter. He tells the Corinthians about his own suffering, his sincerity, his forgiveness, his anxiety about them. He begs them to be honest with him, to love the Lord, to be good to the poor among them, to stop quarreling.

Despite the emotion that runs through the letter, Paul always keeps a tone of authority. He must have felt much as a parent feels toward a child whom he loves dearly even when that child gravely misbehaves and even betrays him. Since the letter contains so many moods and is so highly personal, the reader must try to discover and express the mood(s) of each specific passage.

Ephesians. The early church experienced two major problems: the persecution of Jewish Christians and tension between Christians who were Jewish and those who were Gentile. Paul had worked hard to help the church settle these problems. By the time he wrote this letter, the church had worked through some of the problems and was more united; and Paul was older and calmer. He sounds like a second-generation Christian looking back to difficult beginnings, satisfied that the early crises had been laid to rest. This letter possibly was a "circular" letter, sent not only to Ephesus but also around to other churches. Therefore the tone is not very personal.

The letter should be read calmly, in the spirit of an older man emphasizing the unity and universality of the church. In a sense, it still is a "circular" letter making rounds to present Christian communities.

Galatians. After Paul had worked in Galatia and had left there, Jewish Christians persuaded many of the Gentile Christians that they needed to keep the Jewish law as well as the Christian law. They said that Paul just had not known any better when he said that Gentiles were free from the Judaic law. After all, Paul had not been one of the original twelve apostles!

Paul writes this letter with a bit of fist-shaking frustration and also with an emphatic restatement that Christians are free from the Judaic law and are attached solely to Jesus. In tone, the letter swings from anger to affection; but in either case, the feeling is strong. Notice the dashes and exclamation marks. The letter should be read with passionate intensity and reassurance.

Hebrews. We do not know who wrote this epistle, nor do we know the exact group to which it was written. The letter's style indicates that the author was a Greek-speaking Jew. And the letter's content indicates that it was meant for Christian Jews. Much emphasis is placed on Old Testament prophecies and on the fact that Jesus Christ fulfilled them. This "epistle" probably was a written sermon. It may be effectively read aloud as a well-planned, low-key, educated sermon.

James. This epistle seems to be a written sermon or instruction. It is highly moralistic. James especially warns the people not to settle for a theoretical faith but to put that faith into practice. The word "you" is used a great deal; it gives the letter a very immediate, here-and-now tone. Lectors should read James as if they were delivering a sermon.

I John. This letter clarifies the doctrine of Christ's humanity and divinity, and it stresses concrete Christian love as the witness to that faith. The letter is poetic and has many similarities to John's Gospel. It should be read slowly and with a definite sense of rhythm.

II and III John. These are both very short letters written to specific people. False teachers evidently were in the vicinity, and so it became important that Christians hold very fast to truth. Both letters, then, show the relation of truth and love. And both insist on hospitality toward orthodox missionaries and on rejection of false teachers. The letters are brisk, brief, and to the point.

Jude. Jude wrote this epistle to several Christian communities that suffered danger to their faith and to their moral life. Certain heretics had entered those communities and were encouraging sexual excesses in the name of religion. Jude wrote to encourage the Christians to resist those false teachers and their immoral ways. Jude's epistle has an urgent tone and should be read in an energetic, forceful way.

I Peter. This epistle was written to "scattered strangers" — that is, to small, new communities of Gentile Christians scattered in places where the majority of people were pagan. The epistle evidently was written during a time when these new Christian groups were persecuted by the government and reviled by their pagan neighbors. Peter exhorts them to keep up their courage. He stresses their solidarity as a community; they do not face the problems alone but as a united group. By Baptism, he explains, they became a people of God. That unity should give them courage to live in faith and love despite hardships.

Christians today, in a way, also are "scattered strangers" in the world. The lector should read this letter as an encouragement to them to live more and more as a community of persons united in love through Baptism.

II Peter. Very early Christians thought Christ's second coming would happen any day. After the destruction of Jerusalem in the year 70, they began to realize that the second coming would be much later. For some people, this realization caused a crisis of faith; they thought perhaps that they had misinterpreted the whole Christian teaching. So this epistle reassures the Christians that everything Christ taught is true and that he will indeed come again as he said.

This epistle is very well composed, leading logically from point to point. There is no anger or panic. It should be read in the tone of a teacher trying to clarify a point through a well-prepared lecture.

Philemon. This is a very short, very personal letter to Philemon. It concerns one of Philemon's slaves, Onesimus, who had run away and later had been converted by Paul. In his letter, Paul does not try to abolish the system of slavery but rather the mentality that sees another man as slave. He urges Philemon to receive Onesimus back as a "beloved brother."

Paul wrote this letter while imprisoned in Rome and worn out from his missionary work. The tone of the letter is gentle, warm, personal. The lector's voice should carry those feelings as well as the message.

Philippians. Paul's first European Christian community was at Philippi. The price he paid for that community included arrest, flogging, and imprisonment. But the community flourished, and Paul had a special affection for it. The letter rambles quite a bit; it includes denunciation of Judaizers, news about a mutual sick friend, warnings about false teachers, and concern about his being in prison again and facing trial. Despite its many topics, the letter has a consistent tone of real affection and apostolic joy for those good people at Philippi. It should be read with briskness and optimism and pride.

Romans. The first Christians in Rome were Jews. But the Jews were expelled from there around 40 A.D. After that, it seems that the majority of Christians in Rome were Gentiles. Even though Paul had not yet been to Rome, he was well informed about the community there. He knew, for instance, that certain Jews (called Judaizers) were trying to persuade the Gentile Christians that they had to keep the law of Moses in order to be saved. In this epistle, then, Paul stresses the relationship between Judaism and Christianity, and he explains that Jesus is the new law and the source of salvation.

Paul ordinarily became angered by Judaizers, but in this letter, he keeps his temper. In fact, since he did not know the community personally, the whole letter is emotionally low-keyed. It should be read more like a treatise than a letter.

I Thessalonians. Thessalonia was a Greek city with a large Jewish colony. Paul was rejected by most of the Jews but accepted by some Greeks. These Greek Christians were persecuted by the Jews and the pagan Greeks in Thessalonia. Since Paul's presence made life harder for them, he left. This is his first letter to them after leaving. The community there evidently was strong and steadfast in faith and fervent in charity. The tone of the letter is entirely optimistic and gentle. It should be read proudly and in a commending spirit.

II Thessalonians. Since the Thessalonians — like other early Christians — expected Christ's second coming imminently, they were inclined to be idle. Their thought seemed to be: "Why worry? It'll all be over pretty soon." Coupled with that internal problem was the external problem of intensified persecution. Paul addresses both problems in this second letter to the community at Thessalonia. The letter has a slight scolding tone. It should be read with a voice of authority.

I and II Timothy; Titus. These three pastoral letters are grouped together because they all are addressed to individuals in charge of a local church. (Timothy headed the community at Ephesus; Titus headed the church on the island of Crete.) Those early local churches were beset with misunderstanding and persecution from without and with heresies and misconduct from within. To take charge of a church required moral courage and sure knowledge of the faith as well as leadership and charity. These are the things Paul stresses in these pastoral letters.

The church of the First Century was less organized than the one we know. But the situation nevertheless can be compared to a bishop writing to a priest today serving in a missionary church, endangered by heresy and immorality. Such a letter has concern for the people and trust in the priest.

WORK SHEETS FOR LECTORS

INTRODUCTION

These worksheets for lectors provide learning through involvement. The sheets come to you after having been tested for a year at lectors' worshops around the country. They may be used by the individual or in a group of several persons working together. Our own experience indicates some advantages to the group, or workshop, method. At our workshops, we usually work in groups of four to six. In each small group, the explanations are read aloud, the sheets are worked independently, and then a lively comparison/discussion follows.

After the group sessions, we break to reassemble in the church where each lector has an opportunity to practice handling the lectionary in procession and reading from the lector's stand. The other lectors present help by giving pointers or making suggestions or simply giving pats on the back.

We hope these worksheets help you deepen your relationship with God through the Scriptures and help you read with finer skill and persuasion.

May your reading be happy and holy.

PARAPHRASING

The first and most important way to gain skill in public reading is to make the author's thoughts one's own. Public *speakers* do not have to develop this skill; they speak their own thoughts. But public *readers* do need this skill; they are speaking God's message as given in the words of Paul or Moses or someone else who lived centuries ago. Before that message can be given to believers, lectors must comprehend the message of God and understand something of the author's style and meaning. So making the author's thoughts one's own is the cardinal skill for those public readers called lectors. *Cardinal* means *hinge:* all the other skills that lectors develop hinge on this skill.

The best way to check out your understanding of the author's ideas is to paraphrase the reading. Paraphrasing means not only to express the writer's thoughts in your own words but to try to "get inside" the writer by searching out the circumstances of the writing and the probable feeling of the author. Here is an example from Paul's letter to the Philippians 1:21-24:

For, to me, life means Christ; hence dying is so much gain. If, on the other hand, I am to go on living in the flesh, that means productive toil for me – and I do not know which to prefer.

Background: Paul wrote this from prison. He was probably exhausted by overwork.

Paraphrase: Christ is everything to me. He is really my life! I almost wish I could die because then I could be with him. But I'd also like to go on living for awhile because – even here in this prison – I can still tell people about Christ.

I am strongly attracted to both: I long to be freed from this life and to be with Christ, for that is the far better thing; yet it is urgent that I remain alive for your sakes.

It's a kind of tension inside of me. In one way I'd like to die right now. Nothing would be better than to be with Christ. But in another way, I want more people to get to know him so I'd like to keep on living and keep telling people about Christ.

Lectors may ask: "Where do we get this background? We're not Scripture scholars." It's true, of course, that a good background in Scripture would be most helpful. But if such biblical education is not available or practical, lectors nevertheless can find good help in most Bibles:

1. by reading the entire chapter from which the selection comes, and

2. by reading the introduction to each section of the Bible.

By reading the entire first chapter of the letter to the Philippians, for example, a lector will learn that Paul wrote from prison and that, even in prison, he was spreading the Gospel. And by reading the introduction found in most good translations nowadays, the lector will learn that Paul was imprisoned during his second missionary journey. The hardships of travel in those days plus Paul's tendency to work hard would indicate that he must have been very fatigued.

One final note about the above example of paraphrasing: Notice how the paraphrase is written in the first person — as though the lector *were* Paul. That is what is meant by trying to "get inside" the author.

Exercise 1. Comment on and paraphrase the following
selections. Use your Bible.

A selection from Isaiah 42:5-7:

Thus says God, the Lord,
who created the heavens and
stretched them out,
who spreads out the earth
with its crops,
Who gives breath to its people and spirit to those who
walk on it:
I, the Lord, have called you
for the victory of justice,
I have grasped you by the
hand; I have formed you,
and set you as a light to
the nations, To open the
eyes of the blind to bring
prisoners from confinement
and from the dungeon,
those who live in darkness.

Background: _____

_____

_____

_____

Paraphrase: _____

_____

_____

_____

_____

_____

_____

_____

_____

_____

_____

_____

_____

_____

_____

_____

_____

_____

_____

_____

_____

_____

_____

_____

_____

_____

_____

_____

_____

_____

_____

_____

31

Exercise 2. Selection from the Letter to the Hebrews 5:7-9:

In the days when he was in the flesh, he offered prayers and supplications with loud cries and tears to God, who was able to save him from death and he was heard because of his reverence. Son though he was, he learned obedience from what he suffered; and when perfected, he became the source of eternal salvation for all who obey him.

Background: _____
_____
_____
_____

Paraphrase: _____

PAUSING

Let no one confuse the absence of sound with the absence of meaning. On the contrary. When well planned, *a pause is a silence charged with meaning.* It can motivate listeners to anticipate the next thought, to reflect on the words just finished, to feel, to think, to wonder.

The skill of pausing is dependent on the cardinal skill — or hinge skill — of making the author's thoughts and feelings one's own.

Basically, there are two kinds of pauses. The first is called the *clarification* pause. Clarification pauses usually follow printed punctuation. The second kind of pause is called the *highlight* pause. Highlight pauses add color, meaning, feeling, emphasis. They can make the difference between flat reading and a richer, three-dimensional kind of reading. In adding highlight pauses, lectors will vary depending on what ideas or feelings they intend to emphasize. Study, for example, this reading from Isaiah 42:1-2 with pauses marked differently by two expert lectors.

Here is my servant whom I uphold,/	Here/ is my servant/ whom I uphold,/
my chosen one	my chosen one
with whom I am pleased,//	with whom I am pleased,//
He shall bring forth justice	He shall bring forth/ justice/
to the nations,/	to the nations,//
Not crying out,/ not shouting,/	Not/ crying out,// not/ shouting,//
not making his voice heard	not/ making his voice heard
in the streets.//	in the streets.//

Neither marking is wrong. Both keep the message clear. Yet each marking represents a different style, a different emphasis, dependent on the lector's own style. Notice how the first marking calls for smooth, long phrasing. Notice how the second marking sets off with pauses — and thus emphasizes — the words *justice* and *not.*

To some lectors, long or frequent pauses might seem exaggerated. But it is important to remember that what seems exaggerated in private reading or in reading to a small group does not seem so when the audience is large or when the occasion is formal. In church settings, the audience *is* large and the occasion *is* formal (even in so-called informal liturgies). So lectors have a double reason for slowing the pace of their reading with appropriate pauses.

Exercise 1. Indicate both clarification and highlight pauses in the following selections. Use a single slash (/) for short pauses and double slashes (//) for long pauses.

Selection from 2 Corinthians 5:17-19:

This means that if anyone is in Christ, he is a new creation. The old order has passed away; now all is new! All this has been done by God, who has reconciled us to himself through Christ and has given us the ministry of reconcilia- tion. I mean that God, in Christ, was reconciling the world to himself, not count- ing men's transgressions against them, and that he has entrusted the message of reconciliation to us.

Background: _____

_____

_____

_____

Paraphrase: _____

_____

_____

_____

_____

_____

_____

_____

_____

_____

_____

_____

_____

Exercise 2. Be sure to use the hinge skill of paraphrasing before you determine pauses.

Selection from Micah 5:3:

He shall stand firm and
shepherd his flock by the
    strength of the Lord,
    in the majestic name
    of the Lord, his God;
And they shall remain, for
    now his greatness shall
    reach to the ends of the
    earth;
He shall be peace.

Background: _____
_____
_____
_____

Paraphrase: _____

EMPHASIZING

In ordinary conversation, most people accentuate important words and de-emphasize less important ones. For
some unfortunate reason, this natural inflection is often
lost in oral reading. What is natural in life, then, must be
relearned in art.

Accuracy in meaning depends as much on emphasis
as it does on words. In fact, the same words can have
different meanings when given different emphasis. Thus,
"Are you *jealous*?" does not mean the same thing as "Are
you jealous?"

Meaning, then, depends on the emphasis of certain
words. And emphasis is determined by meaning. So we
are back to the hinge skill: understanding the message
of God and the style of the author. Only then can we
choose appropriate emphases.

In Genesis 41:14-16, for example, the theme, or message, is God's omniscience. That theme is underscored
by the comparison between Joseph and God:

Pharaoh therefore had Joseph summoned, and they
hurriedly brought him from the dungeon. After he
shaved and changed his clothes, he came into Pharaoh's presence. Pharaoh then said to him: "I had
certain dreams that *no one* can interpret. But I
hear it said of *you* that the moment you are told
a dream, you can interpret it." "It is not *I*," Joseph
replied to Pharaoh, "but *God* who will give Pharaoh
the right answer."

Exercise 1. After you have made "the author's thoughts your own," mark both pauses and stresses in the following readings.

Selection from Acts 5:12-15:

Through the hands of the apostles, many signs and wonders occurred among the people. By mutual agreement they used to meet in Solomon's Portico. No one else dared to join them, despite the fact that the people held them in great esteem. Nevertheless more and more believers, men and women in great numbers, were continually added to the Lord. People carried the sick into the streets and laid them on cots and mattresses, so that when Peter passed by, at least his shadow might fall on one or other of them.

Background: _____
_____
_____
_____
Paraphrase: _____
_____
_____
_____
_____
_____
_____
_____
_____
_____
_____
_____
_____
_____
_____
_____
_____
_____
_____
_____
_____
_____
_____
_____
_____
_____
_____

Exercise 2. Selection from Revelations 5:11-14:

I, John, had a vision, and I heard the voices of many angels who surrounded the throne and the living creatures and the elders. They were countless in number, thousands and tens of thousands, and they all cried out:

> "Worthy is the Lamb that was slain to receive power and riches, honor and glory and praise!"

Then I heard the voices of every creature in heaven and on earth and under the earth and in the sea; everything in the universe cried aloud:

> "To the One seated on the throne, be praise and honor, glory and might, forever and ever!"

The four living creatures answered, "Amen," and the elders fell down and worshiped.

Background: _____
_____
_____
_____

Paraphrase: _____
_____
_____
_____
_____
_____
_____
_____
_____
_____
_____
_____
_____
_____
_____
_____
_____
_____
_____
_____
_____
_____
_____
_____
_____
_____
_____
_____
_____
_____
_____
_____

DRAMATIZING

Dramatization refers to a simple change of voice, or key, at appropriate places. This change of key is commonly called "reading with expression." It includes changing mood, pitch, speed. Without this simple kind of dramatization, pauses become mechanical and stresses sound wooden. Then the cardinal rule of proclaiming the message is broken; meaning remains dim.

By the time a conscientious minister of the word searches out some background on a selection, paraphrases it, marks the pauses and stresses, he or she will be fairly certain to know when to put in expression. Even though voice changes usually occur naturally, it might be helpful to indicate some basic rules.

1. Change key when there is a parenthetical comment. Such comments usually are set off with dashes or parentheses. An example (marked *) would be in Philippians 1:3-5:

I give thanks to my God every time I think of you *—which is constantly, in every prayer I utter — rejoicing as I plead on your behalf, at the way you have all continually helped promote the gospel from the very first day.

2. Change key to indicate a change of speakers. An example from 2 Samuel 12:1, 4-6:

The Lord sent Nathan to David, and when he came to him, he said: *"Judge this case for me! In a certain town there were two men, one rich and the other poor. Now, the rich man received a visitor, but he would not take from his own flocks and herds to prepare a meal for the wayfarer who had come to him. Instead he took the poor man's ewe lamb and made a meal of it for his visitor." *David grew very angry with that man and said to Nathan: "As the Lord lives, the man who has done this merits death!"

3. Change key when there is special feeling in the reading. An example would be in the passage from 2 Samuel 12:18-19, when King David's son by Bathsheba dies.

On the seventh day, the child died. David's servants, however, were afraid to tell him that the child was dead. But David noticed his servants whispering among themselves and realized that the child was dead. *He asked his servants, *"Is the child dead?"

4. Change key when there is repetition in Hebrew poetry, typical of the psalms and other poetic pieces in the Bible. Very often an idea in one line is repeated in different words in the following line. The result is a pattern of statement and echo. For example:

I will give thanks to you among the people, O Lord; *I will chant your praise among the nations. For your kindness towers to the heavens, *and your faithfulness to the skies.

After you find some background information and paraphrase the following selections, place an asterisk (*) to
indicate where you would shift key to use a different
expression.

Exercise 1. Selection from Acts
10:1-5:

Background: _____

Now in Caesarea there was a
centurion named Cornelius, of
the Roman cohort Italica, who
was religious and God-fearing.
The same was true of his
whole household. He was in
the habit of giving generously
to the people and he constantly prayed to God. One after-
noon at about three, he had a
vision in which he clearly saw
a messenger of God coming
toward him and calling,
"Cornelius!" He stared at
the sight and said in fear,
"What is it, sir?" The answer came: "Your prayers
and your generosity have
risen in God's sight, and because of them he has remem-
bered you. Send some men
to Joppa and summon a certain Simon, known as Peter."

Paraphrase: _____

Exercise 2. Selection from
Psalm 103:

Bless the Lord, O my soul;
     And all my being, bless
     his holy name.
He pardons all your iniqui-
ties,
     He heals all your ills.

Background: _____

_____

_____

_____

Paraphrase: _____

_____

_____

_____

_____

_____

_____

_____

_____

_____

_____

_____

_____

_____

_____

_____

_____

_____

_____

_____

_____

_____

_____

_____

_____

_____

_____

_____

_____

_____

_____

INTRODUCING

When artists or actors give public readings from, say, a
Shakespearean play, they never just begin reading. They
first make an introduction by telling the name of the
play, the name of the character(s) in the selection, the
situation in which the passage occurs. In short, they
prepare their listeners to receive the reading with understanding and appreciation. Certainly a reading from
God's word deserves as much introduction.

Lectors may include some or all of the following information in an introduction to a scriptural reading:

1. Background on the author.
2. Situation in which the writing was done.
3. Comment on the main theme of the reading.
4. Relation of the reading to the feast or to the
   day's Gospel.

Planning is needed to make an introduction brief yet
clear and interesting. Lectors should write out their introductions. They should make sure that they use a con-
versational tone and make eye contact while giving the introduction. That style — plus a good pause afterwards —
should clearly differentiate the introduction from the
reading itself.

As an example, let us make an introduction for the
following reading from Acts 4:32-35 for the Mass of
the second Sunday of Easter (cycle B):

The community of believers were of one heart
and one mind. None of them ever claimed any-
thing as his own; rather everything was held in
common. With power the apostles bore witness to the resurrection of the Lord Jesus, and
great respect was paid to them all; nor was
there anyone needy among them, for all who
owned property or houses sold them and do-
nated the proceeds. They used to lay them
at the feet of the apostles to be distributed
to everyone according to his need.

The reading could be introduced by either of the following comments:

Short Introduction: In this reading from the Acts of the Apostles, we hear how the early Christians lived the Resurrection of Jesus.

Longer Introduction: A week ago, we celebrated the Resurrection of Jesus. In this reading — from chapter four of the Acts of the Apostles — St. Luke tells us how faith in the Risen Lord prompted the first Christians to share everything they had with one another.

It goes without saying that introductions are planned only after the meaning of a passage has been explored and paraphrased. And so this skill, like the others, hinges on the skill of paraphrasing.

Paraphrase and then write an introduction for the following selections.

Exercise 1. Selection from 2 Corinthians 5:17-20:

This means that if anyone is in Christ, he is a new creation. The old order has passed away; now all is new! All this has been done by God, who has reconciled us to himself through Christ and has given us the ministry of reconciliation. I mean that God, in Christ, was reconciling the world to himself, not counting men's transgressions against them, and that he has entrusted the message of reconciliation to us. This makes us ambassadors for Christ, God as it were appealing through us. We implore you, in Christ's name: be reconciled to God!

Background: _____

_____

_____

_____

Paraphrase: _____

_____

_____

_____

_____

_____

_____

_____

_____

_____

_____

_____

_____

_____

_____

_____

_____

_____

_____

_____

_____

_____

Introductory comment:

_____

_____

_____

_____

_____

_____

Exercise 2. Selection from
Acts 5:

The high priest began the inter-
rogation of the apostles in this
way: "We gave you strict orders not to teach about that
name, yet you have filled Jerusalem with your teaching and
are determined to make us responsible for that man's
blood."

To this, Peter and the
apostles replied: "Better
for us to obey God than
men! The God of our fa-
thers has raised up Jesus
whom you put to death,
'hanging him on a tree.'
He whom God has exalted
at his right hand as a ruler
and savior is to bring re-
pentance to Israel and forgiveness of sins. We testify
to this. So too does the Holy
Spirit, whom God has given
to those who obey him."

Background: _____
_____
_____
_____
_____

Paraphrase: _____
_____
_____
_____
_____
_____
_____
_____
_____
_____
_____
_____
_____
_____
_____
_____
_____
_____
_____
_____
_____
_____

Introductory comment:

_____
_____
_____
_____
_____
_____

PUTTING IT ALL TOGETHER

Since lectors are appointed to *proclaim* God's word,
they should develop as much skill as possible in making
that proclamation resound with faith and energy, conviction and persuasion. The people in the pews depend
on the lector as well as the homilist for their understanding of God's message to them in their here-and-now lives.

The skills of paraphrasing, planning pauses, emphases,
and expression are often two-sided skills: they have a si-
lent side and an oral side. There can be little oral skill
without the ground work explained in this workbook.

After reflecting, paraphrasing, and marking passages,
the lector is ready for oral practice. Try now to bring
all the skills together. First paraphrase and mark the
following readings. Then write an introduction. Final-
ly, practice reading the passage aloud. In your oral practice, give the reading full voice. Try even to exaggerate
the pauses and inflection so that you will feel comfort-
able with the reading.

Exercise 1. Selection from Genesis 15:12-15:

As the sun was about to set, a trance fell upon Abram, and a deep, terrifying darkness enveloped him. Then the Lord said to Abram: "Know for certain that your descendants shall be aliens in a land not their own, where they shall be enslaved and oppressed for four hundred years. But I will bring judgment on the nation they must serve, and in the end, they will depart with great wealth. You, however, shall join your forefathers in peace; you shall be buried at a contented old age."

Introductory comment:

Background: _____

_____

_____

Paraphrase: _____

_____

_____

_____

_____

_____

_____

_____

_____

_____

_____

_____

_____

_____

_____

_____

_____

_____

_____

_____

_____

_____

_____

_____

_____

_____

_____

_____

_____

_____

_____

_____

Exercise 2. Selection from Revelations 21:1-4:

Then I saw new heavens and a new earth. Former heavens and the former earth had passed away, and the sea was no longer. I also saw a new Jerusalem, the holy city, coming down out of heaven from God, beautiful as a bride prepared to meet her husband. I heard a loud voice from the throne call out: "This is God's dwelling among men. He shall dwell with them and they shall be his people and he shall be their God who is always with them. He shall wipe every tear from their eyes, and there shall be no more death or mourning, crying out or pain, for the former world has passed away."

Background: _____
_____
_____
_____

Paraphrase: _____
_____
_____
_____
_____
_____
_____
_____
_____
_____
_____
_____
_____
_____
_____
_____
_____
_____
_____
_____

Introductory comment:
_____
_____
_____
_____
_____
_____
_____

One final word to you as lectors:

**Fear not to cry
and say to the cities of the world:
Here is your God!**

Isaiah 40:9

COMMISSIONING LECTORS

A SUGGESTED RITE

After a homily about the presence of God in the Scriptures and the role of lectors as ministers, the lectors-elect approach the altar. The priest presents them to the people saying:

> (Names), you have been chosen for an important ministry in this parish. We believe that God is truly present in his word. We believe that he becomes present to us in a very special way when his word is read aloud where two or three are gathered in his name.

> Are you willing to take on the ministry of reading God's word to the people of this parish?

> *(I am.)*

> Are you willing to prepare for your ministry by study and prayer before presenting the Word to the people?

> *(I am.)*

The priest then hands a Bible to a representative of the lectors, and he prays:

> God, our Father and Lord, you have given these persons faith in you and in your word. We ask you to help them grow in that faith. We also ask you to speak to us in this community through these ministers. May they realize your word in full joy and knowledge. We ask this in faith. We ask it through your Son, our brother, Jesus Christ.

(This rite may be used during Mass or separately. If the same persons also are being commissioned to distribute the Eucharist, both rites may be joined in one ceremony.)

2620